Original title:
Banana Smoothies and Sunshine

Copyright © 2025 Creative Arts Management OÜ
All rights reserved.

Author: Lorenzo Barrett
ISBN HARDBACK: 978-1-80586-309-0
ISBN PAPERBACK: 978-1-80586-781-4

Refreshing Daybreak

A yellow fruit with a silly grin,
Dancing in the blender, let's begin!
It giggles and swirls like a playful pup,
As it twirls in circles, come on, drink up!

Sipping through a straw, oh what a sight,
A frothy delight, morning feels just right.
With parrot sunglasses, I strut around,
Feeling like royalty, no worries abound.

The kitchen's a circus, laughter fills the air,
Smoothie spills better than a clown's wild flair.
Toss in some berries, let the chaos reign,
Who knew breakfast could drive one insane?

Chasing sunshine, we juggle our cups,
With every sip, life erupts in hiccups.
Joyful and messy, the day has begun,
Let's toast with our mugs, life's sweet and fun!

Joy in Every Drop

A blender roars, a fruit parade,
With yellow cheer, the scene is laid.
Frothy laughter fills the air,
Taste buds dancing, without a care.

Giggles splash like sunny rays,
A drink that brightens cloudy days.
Sip by sip, we share delight,
In every gulp, joy takes flight.

Gleaming Goodness

In a tall glass, sunshine swirls,
A yellow treasure, laughter unfurls.
Dancing spoons, a playful tease,
Come join the fun, it's sure to please.

Chasing lips, the drink is gone,
But giggles linger, carrying on.
Straws like rockets, we take off,
In this sunny world, we laugh and scoff.

Smooth Various

Whirling fruits, a jovial mix,
Creamy dreams, a tasty fix.
With every blend, joys collide,
A fruity adventure we can't hide.

Sipping softly, the world spins round,
Who's the silliest? We debate sound.
Bubbles pop like little jokes,
With slurps and laughs, we're merry folks.

Tropical Daydreams

A sip of summer, laughter flows,
As twisty straws create funny throes.
Mugs of mirth, we hold them high,
In this fruity frolic, spirits fly.

Sunscreen smudged on noses wide,
We giggle as the flavors slide.
Under the warmth, our fancies bloom,
Chasing giggles in the peachy room.

Sunshower Sips

In a glass, a sunny swirl,
Dancing flavors make me twirl.
Fruits with giggles, oh what fun,
Sipping smiles 'til the day is done.

A splash of joy in every gulp,
Like a playful puppy's yelp.
Laughter bubbles, colors bright,
Every sip a pure delight.

Tropical Daydreams

Whirls of color, a fruity blend,
Chasing worries, they all end.
Tropical breezes in a mug,
Every sip a cozy hug.

Coconuts dance on my brain,
When I'm lost in this sweet rain.
Mango laughter fills the air,
In my cup, there's no despair.

Warmth Captured in a Cup

Golden goodness, smooth and neat,
Sipping sunshine, oh so sweet.
With every gulp, the giggles rise,
Blissful heat under clear blue skies.

Chillin' fruit in a frosty mix,
Joyful vibes in every fix.
Blend my worries, fill with cheer,
Cheers to happiness right here!

Golden Fusion

Twists of sweetness swirl in cheer,
Mingle bold flavors, have no fear.
Sips of sunshine, zesty zing,
In my glass, the joy I bring.

Gleeful giggles, a tasty spree,
Each smooth sip a big "Whee!"
Blends of joy and fruity fun,
With every sip, I've already won.

Summer Solstice Sips

In a jar with a twist, cold and bright,
A drink that dances in morning light.
Whirls of joy with every slurp,
Taste buds jump, hearts do the chirp.

In shades of yellow, a playful mix,
With giggles and grins, it's pure bliss tricks.
Straw hats bobbing, laughter flows,
As sweet sunshine sings, everybody knows.

Radiant Daybreaks

Wake up early, the kitchen's a show,
A blender's roar, watch it go!
Creamy delight blended so fine,
Morning antics with a twist of lime.

Sunbeams peek through each window frame,
While fruity chaos calls our name.
Splash in some chuckles, toss in some cheer,
Sip 'n sip more, let's spread the good cheer!

Vibrant Gold

Golden swirls in a glass so tall,
Giggles erupt as some start to fall.
Pour it greener, add laughter a lot,
Summer sips ready, let's give it a shot!

A dance of flavors, a frothy parade,
Every gulp brings a new charade.
Silly straws twist, we wear them with pride,
In fruity adventures, we shall ride!

Sunshine Embrace

A splash of cheer in every cup,
Raise your glass, let's all erupt!
With sun-kissed smiles, oh what a thrill,
Sip by sip, oh joy we spill.

Joyful notes in a fruity tune,
Flinging shade under a bright balloon.
As laughter rolls like warm summer breeze,
Let's drink to wacky, silly memories, please!

Brilliant Mornings

In the morning glow, a yellow delight,
A swirl of cheer, what a funny sight!
Wobbling cups on the counter stand,
Laughter spills like grains of sand.

Sipping joy with a goofy grin,
Who knew breakfast could be such a win?
A splash of cream, a twist of fun,
A giggle, a wiggle, the day's begun!

Nature's Sip of Joy

Beneath the trees, a drink so bright,
Leaves dance around in pure delight.
With each slurp, a funny song,
Nature's cup, where we all belong.

Playful drops on our noses land,
We giggle aloud, how silly we stand!
Frothy dreams in a wild swirl,
In every sip, a twist to unfurl.

Chasing Light

Hustling down the street, feeling spry,
A fruity potion catches the eye.
Friends chuckle at the silly spill,
Chasing beams, oh what a thrill!

With every swirl, the sun beams bright,
Joyful chaos in delicious bites.
We toast to the day with our merry drinks,
In witty banter, our laughter links.

Twilight Chill

As the day fades, we wave goodbye,
Golden mustaches under the sky.
Laughter echoes as shadows play,
Fruity giggles, let's dance away!

In twilight hues, the glasses clink,
Sweet sips that make us think.
A funny tale on the night's cool breeze,
With every laugh, our hearts feel ease.

Tropical Whispers

In a glass of yellow cheer,
Swirls of laughter, oh so clear.
Fuzzy straws and silly sips,
Joyful giggles as it drips.

Tropical dreams in every pour,
Mischief dancing, begging for more.
With each sip, the sunbeams hop,
Eager tongues that never stop.

Golden Mornings in a Glass

Morning magic blended bright,
Creamy swirls that feel just right.
Sipping smiles, a goofy grin,
Nutty giggles swirl within.

Glorious warmth in every taste,
Chasing off the morning haste.
Laughter bubbles in a whirl,
A fruity dance, a happy swirl.

Creamy Bliss of Summer

Creamy cups and crazy straws,
Summer giggles without pause.
Frothy fun in every gulp,
Joyful hearts begin to lulp.

Chillin' with my fruity brew,
Silly antics, just us two.
Twist and twirl, the fun won't end,
As sunlit splashes make us grin.

Citrus Kisses at Dawn

Zesty zings that tickle taste,
Morning smiles we can't waste.
Fruity flavors that collide,
In our cups, the joy will bide.

Silly faces, sunny beams,
Mingling laughter, joyful screams.
Wake up bright and sip away,
With every taste, a bright parade.

Vibrant Vibes

In a glass so cheerful and bright,
Fruits dance and laugh in pure delight.
Silly straws in a swirling spin,
Giggling flavors, let the fun begin!

Whipped cream clouds float on top,
Sipping joy till you pop!
Fruits do a jig, in fruity parade,
A smoothie party, all worries fade!

Serene Sips

With every gulp, the world slows down,
Chill vibes float, nothing wears a frown.
Smooth blends swirl like a gentle breeze,
Bring me laughter, one sip, and I'm pleased.

Witty flavors tickle the tongue,
In this creamy world, I feel so young.
Each sip sings a happy tune,
Who knew joy could be a drink at noon?

Sun-kissed Delights

Gold in a cup, radiates cheer,
A splash of laughter, nothing to fear.
Fruits frolic, mixing in harmony,
Sips so sweet, they're pure comedy!

Bright sunshine beams through every sip,
Chasing away gloom, on this joy trip.
Each bubble bursts with a giggle large,
In this fruity ride, I'm the captain in charge!

Creamy Sunshine Dreams

A frothy swirl of cheer and cream,
This joy ride feels like a happy dream.
Scoops of bliss in a playful dance,
Sip by sip, I'm lost in the romance.

Cherries on top make a funny face,
Join the party, let's pick up the pace!
Creamy smiles soft as a cloud,
In every sip, I sing out loud!

Sunlit Elixirs

In a glass, a golden swirl,
Frothy dreams begin to twirl.
Sip it slow, don't let it spill,
Giggles rise, it's quite a thrill!

A twist of fruit, a splash of cheer,
They'll melt your worries, never fear.
With every gulp, the sunbeam gleams,
Life's a laughter, or so it seems.

Fruity Reverie

Chilling drinks that dance and hum,
Stirring up a tasty drum.
A playful laugh, a fruity fare,
Each sip sings, without a care.

A splash of giggles, oh so sweet,
Feel the joy with every treat.
The world a canvas, bright and fun,
With zesty sips, our day is won!

Joyful Sips of Radiance

Bubbly brews that tease the tongue,
Soft as songs that are half-sung.
Swirling whirls of sheer delight,
Mixing laughter, pure and bright!

Catch the flavors, let them flow,
In sunlight's warmth, we dance and glow.
Gulp it down, feel the glee,
Silly smiles, just you and me.

Dancing in the Light

A zany twist, a fruit parade,
Cups held high, no time to fade.
Juicy tides of summer's best,
Chasing down sweet happiness!

Lemon drops and laughter rings,
While goofy folks do silly things.
In bubbles, joy and sunshine meet,
Let's raise our cups and take a seat!

Luscious Layers

A twist of yellow, oh what a sight,
Swirling and blending, pure delight.
Chuckles abound with each tasty sip,
 Giggles arise, let happiness rip.

Fruits in a whirl, a carnival dance,
Bright flavors collide, giving taste buds a chance.
Sipping so slowly, with a grin so wide,
 Who knew a drink could be such a ride?

Morning Light Fusions

A splash of joy, early in the morn,
With each little slurp, hear laughter adorn.
A frothy concoction, so creamy and bright,
Miracles in mugs, what a funny sight!

Mixing up giggles, right out of the jar,
Each gulp of delight, it's a flavor bazaar.
Bubbles of laughter, all filled with glee,
If only the world could sip joy like me!

Sunkissed Indulgence

A sunny embrace in a chilled, fruity glass,
Laughter erupts, like a comic class.
Chipper and cheerful, with flavors that dance,
This sipping excitement puts boredom in a trance.

Lemon twists giggle, alongside creamy cheer,
What fun little flavors—with friends ever near!
Taste buds unite, in this frosty caper,
Chasing away dreariness, no room for a graper!

Zesty Sunrise Swirls

A playful shimmer, in every bright sip,
Furry little smiles, let merriment rip.
Bright yellow joy, with a hint of zest,
This funny concoction, truly the best!

Splashing and clashing, a comic delight,
Each twirl brings giggles, morning feels right.
With each goofy gulp, I can't help but beam,
Join in this madness, sip into a dream!

Brightened Mornings

In a blender, fruits collide,
With giggles and a splash inside.
Yellow mush, oh what a sight,
A morning drink, pure delight!

Stirring joy in every cup,
Funny faces, cheers go up.
Sip it slow, or gulp it fast,
Laughter in each sip amassed.

Cozy Sunshine Vibes

A frothy drink, oh what a treat,
Sippin' slow, it can't be beat.
Through the window, rays all gleam,
A smoothie love, the perfect dream!

Mustache of foam, it's quite a scene,
Giggles burst, like bubbles, keen.
Chill out here, let worries slide,
Sipping joy, laughter our guide.

Savoring Sun

Fruits in hand, a silly pose,
Laughter bubbles, goodness flows.
Frosty mix, a funny dance,
Take a sip, now's your chance!

Bubbles pop, as jokes abound,
Joyful moments all around.
Ripened sweetness, sunshine cheer,
Blend it well, let's persevere!

Golden Glow

Whirls of yellow, giggles roar,
Each gulp feels like a sunny score.
Fruity mustaches, smiles so wide,
A golden glow, we sip with pride!

Dance with flavors, swirl and twist,
Funny faces, none can resist.
Chilled delight, let's laugh and cheer,
With every sip, our joy is clear!

Radiance in a Bowl

In a kitchen bright with laughter,
A splash of yellow, what a game!
Mixing joy in a big blender,
Fruits dance 'round, no one to blame.

Straws in hand, we sip with glee,
Caught in a fruity, frothy bliss.
We peel away all our worries,
And giggle with each tasty kiss.

The blender roars like a concert,
Music of sweetness fills the air.
Each gulp's a burst of pure rapture,
As we sip without a care.

With smiles wide and hearts so light,
We toast to flavors, wild and free.
In this bowl, pure delight,
Our silly tales are meant to be.

Beachy Smoothies

On sandy shores, the sunbeam shines,
A kaleidoscope of bright delight.
We blend the fruity summertime,
With splashes of laughter, oh what a sight!

Pineapple makes a goofy face,
While mango swirls in a dance so sweet.
The blender churns with joyful grace,
As surf and smoothies find their beat.

Ice cubes crash like waves in cheer,
Each sip's a ticket to the fun.
With sunny smiles all around here,
We sip until the day is done.

The jokes flow too, like ocean tides,
As fruity colors twirl and twine.
We cheer for life, with goofy guides,
In every glass, our spirits shine.

Sunbeam Nectar

Golden rays hug our glasses tight,
In a whirl of taste, we take our shot.
Laughter bubbles, oh what a sight,
With fruity treasures, we sip a lot.

A splash of zest from zestful fruits,
Mixing in bubbles, vibes so bright.
We giggle as this blend takes roots,
Creating joy in every bite.

Tasting the sunshine, it zings delight,
Each sip a chuckle, a ticklish tease.
Silly faces brought to light,
With every gulp, we laugh with ease.

The blender roars, a comic scene,
Chasing worries, one sip away.
In this nectar, we find the sheen,
Sunbeam jokes brighten up our day.

Whirlwind of Flavor

A blender spins, a fruity flight,
Twirling flavors, oh what a spark!
Lemons chuckle, berries unite,
Crafting joy in a frothy arc.

With silly straws, we take a drink,
A giggle-coated sip of bliss.
Each swirl a chance to stop and think,
Are these flavors just a sweet kiss?

Whirls of color, pure surprise,
A carnival ride in our cups.
With laughter echoing through the skies,
We toast our thrills and happy hiccups.

In this chaos, joy's the prize,
With every sip, we burst out loud.
Finding fun with the silliest ties,
In our tasty whirlwind, we feel proud.

Daybreak Delight

Morning giggles fill the air,
Yellow blenders dance with flair.
Sips of joy, oh what a treat,
Chasing clouds, can't feel my feet.

Lemon laughter, citrus cheer,
Peeling fruit, I've naught to fear.
Spoon on standby, got no shame,
In this smoothie-making game.

Sticky fingers, splashes bright,
Crafting breakfast, pure delight.
Straws like umbrellas in a flight,
Whirling colors, what a sight!

The kitchen's chaos makes me grin,
Each blend a giggle, let's begin!
Ripe and ready, fruit parade,
Time for joy, let's make a trade!

Fresh and Fruity Mornings

Dawn awakens, laughter spills,
Fruit parade through morning hills.
Whipped up mischief, oh what fun,
Chasing rays until we're done.

Joking with the mango zest,
Yogurt's got a playful jest.
Slippers slide on kitchen tiles,
Fruity explosions bring the smiles.

Bubbles pop in sips we share,
Blenders whirl with fruity flair.
Harvesting giggles with a twist,
Mirthful mornings, can't resist!

Peel back laughter, find the gold,
Fictional tales of fruit so bold.
With every gulp, the sun awakes,
Silly joy in fruity lakes!

Harvest of Joy

Bouncing berries in a bowl,
Chasing laughter, that's the goal.
Peachy whispers in the breeze,
Tweaking flavors, if you please.

Frothy wonders, twist and spin,
Morning melodies begin to grin.
Every sip, a bubbly cheer,
Finding smiles as the sun draws near.

Fruits unite in swirling dance,
Juggling flavors, take a chance!
Sipping sunshine, hugs so warm,
Joyful harvest, perfect charm.

Lively concoctions, tasty treats,
Laughter rings as each one beats.
With a splash, the day begins,
In fruity fun, the heart just wins!

Whimsical Whirls

Twisty tales in cups I see,
Wiggly fruit, oh joy and glee.
Whirling smiles in shades so bright,
Sip by sip, we take to flight.

Lively mixes make me sing,
Dancing flavors, what joy they bring.
Flashy straws in a fruity race,
Every sip's a warm embrace.

Giggly chunks in golden dreams,
Smoothing out the morning schemes.
With each blend, our laughter soars,
Fruity puddles on the floors!

Each swirl a glimpse of sunlit play,
Merry moments in disarray.
In bubbly joy we find our way,
Whimsical whirls make our day!

Sunlit Sips

In a cup so bright and yellow,
A frothy swirl, a bouncing jello,
With giggles mixed, a smoothie dance,
Each sip a sunny, playful chance.

A straw that bends, it winks at me,
Oh what a sight, so full of glee,
I tip my head, a funny grin,
As fruity flavors burst within.

The blender roars, it whirs and spins,
A kitchen concert, everyone wins,
Each drop a laugh, a summer prank,
A joyful blend, we boldly drank.

So raise your cup, give a cheer,
For cheerful tastes that bring us near,
The sun shines bright, the day is fine,
In every sip, the joy is mine.

Creamy Morning Rays

Awake to joy, the sun aglow,
A creamy dream, it starts to flow,
With chuckles sweet, and a wink so sly,
I swear I saw a fruit fly by.

The blender hums a silly tune,
As I mix in tales of the afternoon,
A splash of giggles, a dash of cheer,
Makes every sip a treasure here.

My cup is full, it sings so bright,
A funny twist that feels just right,
Each swirl a smile, a laugh that bounces,
In morning rays, my spirit flounces.

So gather round, friends, it's time to sip,
The fruity fun, don't let it slip,
With creamy joy, the day we seize,
A sunlit feast that aims to please.

Fruitful Whispers

In a whirl of fruit, the laughter flows,
A drink so silly, everyone knows,
Each whisper sweet, a punchline trial,
In every sip, a fruity smile.

A giggle here, a chuckle there,
As juicy colors fill the air,
With every gulp, we burst with fun,
A slippery chase, we all just run.

Lime and mint join the quirky band,
A smoothie stage, oh, isn't it grand?
Each fruity blend, a quirky tale,
Like dancing sticks in a vibrant gale.

So take a sip, let laughter fly,
In every cup, our joy will lie,
With whispered jokes and fruity cheer,
We celebrate this tasty year.

Bright Daydreams

Chasing sunbeams in a fruity haze,
I sip and grin through golden rays,
Each taste a tickle, a playful prank,
With every gulp, my spirits flank.

A twist of fun, the flavors tease,
In creamy pools, we float with ease,
With silly straws that bend and curl,
We laugh and munch, a summer swirl.

From berry bursts to citrus smiles,
Our glasses clink through all the miles,
In bright daydreams, we're full of cheer,
With fruity gigs, let's persevere.

So sip with joy, don't let it end,
In laughter's glow, we will transcend,
A banquet bright, a juicy feast,
In every hug, our smiles released.

Elixirs of the Warmth

In a glass so tall and bright,
Yellow whirlwinds take to flight.
With every sip, a giggle steals,
A tropical dance that whirls and squeals.

Straws bend like they're doing tricks,
Sipping joy, it's all in the mix.
Giggles bubble, flavors collide,
Creamy laughter in every stride.

Sunshine shines, gleefully gold,
Warmth in each sip, stories untold.
Slurping sounds, what a fine tune,
Under bright skies, we're over the moon.

So grab a cup, join the fun spree,
In a swirl of flavors, come dance with me!
Let's toast to joy, in every swirl,
Elixirs of laughter, let's give it a whirl!

Fruity Daydreams

In fruity lands where giggles roam,
A creamy cloud is my new home.
Swirls of joy in every cup,
With every sip, I'm ready to sup.

Fruits frolic, twirling around,
In my drink, sweet jests abound.
Jokes and flavors in a fun parade,
Every sip, a laughter cascade.

Bubbles bounce, a circus cheer,
Funny hats and light-hearted beer.
With every taste, my worries drain,
A fruity daydream, oh, what a gain!

So keep the blender on full blast,
In a whirl of joy, let's have a blast!
Laughing together, our cares will flee,
In this fruity wonder, just you and me!

Golden Bliss in the Breeze

Waves of flavor dance in tune,
Golden treasures, a taste of June.
Sunshine smiles in every blend,
As cheerful sips around us wend.

Chasing clouds with spoons of glee,
Each creamy drop, a jubilee.
Silly stories from sunny lands,
Caught in flavor, we make our plans.

Laughter spills, sweet and bright,
Joyful rhythms, pure delight.
In every glass, a comic twist,
A splash of fun that can't be missed.

Together we sip and share our dreams,
Breezy giggles, golden beams.
Forever joyful, in laughter's seize,
We toast our treats on the warmest breeze!

Sunkissed Indulgence

Waking up in a citrus delight,
Sunkissed goodness, oh what a sight!
Frothy blushes in every bowl,
A funny feast to lift the soul.

Giggles swirl like a creamy tide,
Fruity flavors, we cannot hide.
With every slurp, a laughter burst,
In this fun game, we're always first.

Dancing flavors, tickling the tongue,
Sweet jests as bright as songs unsung.
Let's guzzle joy, let cheer reside,
In this blend of fun, we take pride.

So raise your cups, let laughter reign,
In our sunkissed world, we'll entertain!
Blend the happiness, let spirits flow,
In this indulgence, we steal the show!

Nectar of the Dawn

Morning delight in a glass,
A yellow swirl, a fruity blast.
Straws like swords in a liquid fight,
Sipping giggles 'til it's night.

Mustache of froth on my nose,
Sticky fingers from fruity prose.
Laughter bubbles in each pour,
Refills coming, but I want more!

Bouncing flavors, a silly dance,
Whirling joy with each new chance.
Chasing sunshine in every sip,
A creamy journey, a joyful trip.

When life feels dull, give it a whirl,
This zesty drink will make you twirl.
With each guffaw and every cheer,
The world's much brighter, that is clear!

Cheerful Chillers

Fruits collide in a merry mix,
Slushy giggles and fruity tricks.
Twists and turns in a frosty spin,
Drink it down, let the fun begin.

Cousin Larry's ticklish grin,
As he sips, a spin begins.
Sticky giggles, splat and slosh,
It's a wacky, fruity bonanza, posh!

A blender dance with a rumble loud,
Crushing ice like a silly crowd.
Who knew a drink could bring such glee?
Joy in a cup is the best, you see!

Laughter twirls like a beach ball toss,
With every gulp, we're at a loss.
For words to describe this frothy bliss,
Sipping happiness is pure happiness!

Radiant Refreshments

A glass of yellow magic swirls,
Fruity dreams and giggles whirl.
Lemon drops with a cheeky tease,
Every sip is sure to please.

Sunshine smiles in a frosty cup,
Lifting spirits, up, up, up!
Sips so sweet, they make you grin,
A zesty twist in a playful spin.

Joyful jests come with each blend,
Like a party where the fun won't end.
Guffaws erupt while we toast and sip,
With fruity flavors that make us flip.

When the world feels gray and cold,
This vibrant drink breaks the mold.
With a burst of laughter and pure delight,
Life's a party, hold on tight!

Smooth Sailing in Citrus

A twist of zest on a sunny day,
Fruity waves come out to play.
In a frothy boat, we glide with glee,
Chugging down our glassy sea.

With a whirl and a giggle, we blend,
Fizzy vibes are our best friend.
Orange fluff and a splash of cheer,
Whoa! It just kicked into high gear!

Oceans of smiles, sailing free,
Each gulp a ticket to jubilee.
Like cartoon ducks, we honk and quack,
Who knew fruity fun had no knack?

Happiness floats on a creamy tide,
In this wild ride, we all collide.
Smooth sailing's here, our spirits soar,
Grab a glass, let's laugh some more!

Golden Harvest

In a blender, fruits collide,
Whirling chaos, nothing to hide.
Splashes of yellow, sticky delight,
Maybe a smoothie for breakfast or night.

Sipping slowly, it sloshes around,
Laughter bubbles, a silly sound.
With each gulp, the giggles grow,
Who knew a drink could steal the show?

Straws like umbrellas in a fizzy sea,
Chilling vibes, just you and me.
A taste that dances atop your tongue,
Let's raise a toast, we're forever young.

As we blend and sip with glee,
Who needs a forest? We've got a tree.
So grab a cup, and let's get loud,
In our fruity world, we're forever proud.

Breezy Bliss

Whipping cream with a splash of cheer,
Sunshine in a glass, crystal clear.
Fruits party on a spinning plate,
Grab your straw, let's celebrate!

Twirling flavors, a playful tease,
Giggling as we sip with ease.
A tropical splash in every swirl,
Life's a dance, give it a twirl!

Fuzzy peaches and a laugh or two,
Chasing the worries, it's just me and you.
The kitchen's a mess, but what's the rush?
We've crafted a brew, let's feel the hush.

Through straw-shaped breezes, we sway and sip,
Watch out world, it's a funny trip!
In every gulp, joy takes its flight,
Under the gaze of golden light.

Twilight in a Jar

Evening potions, a sight to adore,
Laughter mixed with fruit galore.
Twilight whispers in a crazy blend,
Sipping sweet while giggles transcend.

The blender's roar, a comedic thrill,
Each spin a joke, we can't keep still.
Shadows dance as we make our treat,
Twilight's magic can't be beat.

Sipping slowly under starry skies,
A splash of laughter, a bit of surprise.
Delightful chaos in every sip,
With fruity colors, let's take a trip.

In a jar of dreams, let's play and cheer,
Craving fun and flavors, never fear.
With a cheeky grin, take a bold leap,
In this wacky moment, we'll never sleep!

Sweet Sunlit Moments

Jumping jugs of joy, oh what a sight,
Chasing flavors, feeling so bright.
Sippin' sunshine, smiles are wide,
Good times frolic, let's take a ride.

Fridge door swings, a fruity spree,
Mix and mash, just you and me.
Cherries giggle, and oranges dance,
Join the fun, it's a smoothie romance!

Slurping slow, giggles rise high,
With slippery straws, oh me, oh my!
Hit repeat, life's a tasty dream,
Sun-kissed moments with a fruity theme.

Let the world whirl, we'll stand right here,
With our merry drinks and no hint of fear.
Cheers to the fun and laughter we find,
In every sip, peace of mind.

A Symphony of Flavors

In a blender, fruits collide,
With giggles and grins, they glide.
The splatters dance, a fruity play,
As flavors sing, they sway away.

Oh, the madness of creamy swirls,
As laughter bubbles in a whirl.
A splash of joy, a twist of zest,
In every sip, a happy jest.

Chillin' out, we take a sip,
Around the kitchen, we all slip.
With every gulp, the fun grows wide,
A taste parade we can't abide!

Blend it, slurp it, make it loud,
We cheer for froth, we cheer aloud.
In this fruity feast, we're all the stars,
With crazy tastes from near and far!

Liquid Sunshine

A splash of cheer, a cup of glee,
With giggles bright, we guzzle free.
Every sip, a cheeky grin,
Happy vibes, let the fun begin!

Swirling flavors dance so bright,
A sip of joy, pure delight.
Take a sip, and watch us beam,
We're all caught in this fruity dream!

The blender roars, a playful sound,
As drippy joy flies all around.
Messy smiles and sticky palms,
In this moment, life's full of charms!

Raise your glasses, let's toast high,
To fruity floods and laughter's sky.
In this swirl of liquid bliss,
We find our happy, juicy kiss!

Creamy Daybreak

Morning breaks with a fruity splash,
In the blender, watch it thrash.
Creamy dreams in cheerful dance,
With every sip, we take a chance.

Chillin' fruits, a playful blend,
Silly shouts, around the bend.
With laughter loud, we raise our cups,
In this zany morning up!

The blender's roar, a silly song,
We mix and chunk, can't go wrong.
Orange giggles, and fruity fun,
Our creamy masterpiece is on the run!

In every sip, a taste so bold,
With silly faces, stories told.
Messy mornings, laughter spreads,
With creamy dreams filling our heads!

Harvest of Happiness

Gather 'round for a fruity feast,
From plump delights, we take a least.
Silly straws in every hand,
In this playful, tasty land.

Frothy giggles in every cup,
Round and round, we down the sup.
With each blend, a chuckle brews,
Of wacky flavors, we can't refuse!

Messy fun that fills the air,
As fruity madness takes us where?
In flavors swirling, jokes abound,
This harvest leaves us joyfully drowned!

So raise your cups, let laughter ring,
In every sip, the joy we bring.
With sneaky smiles and creamy bliss,
Let's toast to fruity moments like this!

Sun-drenched Delicacies

In a cup of yellow cheer,
Twirling flavors, oh so clear,
With a splash of laughter too,
I smile as I sip my brew.

Fruits dancing in a swirl,
Making taste buds feel the whirl,
Sprinkles of joy on top abound,
Happiness in each sip found.

Giggles blend with fruity tales,
As the sun shines, never fails,
A creamy dream that's pure delight,
Chasing shadows, feeling bright.

Mornings shine with playful zest,
Every sip, it feels like a jest,
With each slurp, my grin extends,
A wacky brew that never ends.

Exotic Twirls

Whirls of color fill my glass,
Tropical friends in a funky mass,
I sip with glee, and then I find,
Joy is mixed, and well-defined.

With each gulp, giggles arise,
Tastes of laughter fill the skies,
A hint of mischief, a twist of fun,
Every sip's a silly run.

Fruits from lands both far and near,
Join the party, bring good cheer,
In this funky, fruity whirl,
Life feels like a merry twirl.

Silly straws and winky eyes,
A smoothie world, no need for ties,
We blend and dance in fruity tunes,
Chasing away the afternoon.

Heavenly Fusion

A creamy wave, a fruity tide,
In a cup, good vibes collide,
With laughter sprinkles on the top,
I sip and giggle, never stop.

Coconuts and berries play,
Mixing colors in a ray,
It's a party, just beware,
One sip might float you in the air.

The blender's whirring, what a sound,
Flavor fiesta all around,
In this bowl of whimsy bright,
Every taste feels just right.

Sipping joy in every drop,
Fruity fun that never flops,
Life's too short not to indulge,
In this fusion, hearts will bulge.

Blissful Savor

In my cup, a sunny giggle,
Joyful flavors make me wiggle,
Every slurp sends smiles afloat,
With fruity sails, my spirit's gloat.

Silly faces, laugh parade,
With every sip, my cares do fade,
Frosted fun that chills my soul,
A tasty treat that makes me whole.

Wiggly straws in playful fights,
Who can drink with all their might?
Wacky games and fruity sips,
A carnival that never quits.

Under the sky, we raise our cups,
In this moment, laughter erupts,
A blend of fun, a joyful favor,
Each sip brings bliss to savor.

Sunshine in a Glass

I blended up a yellow hue,
With giggles in a cup, it's true.
The blender roars, my fruit parade,
Laughter's the secret, I'm unafraid.

A splash of joy, a twist of glee,
Who knew the blender could be so free?
With swirling joy and fruity cheer,
I sip the sun, it's bright and clear.

Joyful Blends

In my kitchen, chaos reigns,
Fruits are dancing, skipping lanes.
A scoop of giggles, sprinkle of fun,
Blend it all, oh what have I spun?

Stirred with humor, laughter flows,
Each sip a burst, that's how it goes.
I raise my glass, cheers fill the air,
Joyful concoctions, beyond compare.

Golden Mornings

Awake to sunshine, a blend I crave,
In my cup, there's a cheerful wave.
Fruit in a frenzy, frolic and sway,
Golden delights that brighten my day.

Mix in some giggles, stir with a grin,
Sipping on laughter, let the fun begin.
Every gulp tickles, a joyful spree,
Morning magic, wild and free.

Liquid Sunshine

A whirl of color, a splash of cheer,
This cup of joy is finally here.
Sip and slurp, the giggles start,
A smoothie smile warms my heart.

Each yummy gulp, a funny joke,
In liquid form, my bliss awoke.
Sunshine in flavors, oh what a scene,
A drink so sweet, it's a daytime dream.

Sweet Reveries under Clear Skies

In a world where fruits unite,
A yellow fruit danced in delight.
With splashes of cream, oh what a sight,
We blend and whisk till stars shine bright.

Laughter spills with every pour,
Each sip is joy, we crave for more.
Bubbles giggle, flavors soar,
A whimsical treat we all adore.

Giggling under sun's warm rays,
We sip our dreams in sunny bays.
Each frothy bite in happy phase,
Life tastes sweeter on our play days.

So raise your glasses, cheer a toast,
To fruity fun, our silly boast.
In every slurp, we dance and coast,
Forever craving what we love most.

Savoring the Glow

A splash of yellow in a glass,
Lemon drops fall, the flavors amass.
Giggles bubble — oh, what a class,
As fruit takes flight, this party's a blast!

Sipping slowly, we start to sway,
Each sip a giggle, come what may.
In sunshine's arms, we laugh and play,
With fruity joy, we can't delay.

Creamy swirls in a sunshine dance,
With every slurp, we take a chance.
Bright hues of happiness enhance,
In flavors bold, we make romance.

So let's embrace this tasty spree,
Where laughing's easy, something free.
In every blend, a memory,
Together in giggles, you and me.

Tropical Bliss

In a tropical land where tastes collide,
A fruit parade witters with pride.
Creamy waves and giggles glide,
In joyous sips, together we ride.

Sipping sunshine from a fancy cup,
With wild flavors that erupt.
Each frosted drop just lifts us up,
Filling us with giggles, oh so abrupt.

A splash of fun in every swirl,
Watch as fruity flavors twirl.
Laughter erupts, it's quite the whirl,
As joy cascades, our hearts unfurl.

So come, my friends, embrace the fun,
In this sunshine blast, we're all as one.
With frothy bliss and giggles spun,
Let's drink to laughter—our day's begun!

Golden Elixirs

Within the kitchen, magic brews,
Golden treasures, we can't refuse.
A frothy mix of giggles ensues,
Each sip a burst of summer blues.

We gather round with cups held high,
Each golden swirl makes spirits fly.
With silly faces and a gleam in our eye,
A concoction made for the fun nearby.

Pouring laughter like a rainbow stream,
With creamy sprinkles, we can't help but beam.
In every taste, we scheme and dream,
Elixirs of joy, our hearts supreme.

So toast to flavors that make us grin,
With golden wonders, let's begin.
In every sip, we find the win,
A fruity journey, let the fun begin!

Liquid Joy

A yellow drink with a frothy grin,
Twirling straw, let the slurping begin.
Giggles bubble as it swirls about,
Pour me more, without a doubt!

Fruits are dancing in a happy blend,
Whispering secrets, they start to bend.
Ticklish taste buds request a treat,
Sipping laughter feels so sweet.

Clouds of cream float in the mix,
Tasty tributes to childhood tricks.
Each icy sip, a giggle spree,
Come join the fruity jubilee!

A party in a cup, oh what a sight,
Pour a little joy, feel the delight.
What's your flavor, come take a chance,
In this kooky, fruity dance!

Lively Layers

A splash of color in a tall glass tower,
Frothy fun that gives me power.
Every sip's a silly thrill,
Wobble on, can't sit still!

Strawberry laughter mixed with a twist,
Creamy dreams, should I resist?
Oh no, a brain freeze hits me quick,
But forgot the pain, it's just too slick!

Mirthful bubbles pop in glee,
Flavors playing hide and seek.
With every gulp, I'm feeling brave,
Splashing fun, like a playful wave!

A vibrant swirl like a carnival fair,
Sweet madness flowing through my hair.
With each gulp a chuckle or two,
A layered laugh that's never blue!

Mellow Sunshine

A creamy hug on a sunny day,
Drizzle of joy in the silliest way.
Pineapple whispers, coconut grins,
Let the laughter begin again!

Chunky sips that whisper ease,
Throw in some giggles, if you please.
Chillin' out in a fruity tide,
Empty glasses? Let's not hide!

Promises of sweetness and cheer,
Sip until all worries disappear.
Frothy tops with a sparkle divine,
Life's just better with this sunshine!

Raise those glasses, let's toast aloud,
To fruity fun, let's draw a crowd.
In every gulp, there's a silly rhyme,
Mellow moments, every time!

Sunkissed Splendor

A zesty splash brings out the fun,
Whirling colors in the sun.
Laughter bubbles, flavors collide,
Sip away, let joy reside!

Every swirl is a party call,
In a cup that's big and tall.
Magic mix, no space for gloom,
Chasing troubles straight to the tomb!

With whipped cream hats and cherry crowns,
We're sipping giggles, laughing sounds.
A vibrant dance in a glass so bright,
Stay a while, it feels so right!

So raise your glass, don't sip alone,
In sunkissed splendor, we've brightly grown.
Share a laugh, share a cheer,
With each slurp, we'll conquer fear!

Liquid Rays of Joy

A yellow drink with a twist,
A fruity blend, how could we miss?
Sipping joy in the warm, warm glow,
Dancing with each sip, oh what a show!

With goofy straws and frothy smiles,
We giggle, sip, and run for miles.
The fruits all smiling in our cups,
Swirling laughter, mixing ups!

Lemonade laughs in a fruity race,
Each gulp tickles, what a funny place!
A splash of cheer in every round,
With silly faces, that joy is found!

Pouring sunshine, bursting bright,
Who knew sipping could feel so right?
With friends around, what a delight,
In our cups, the world feels light!

A Blend of Brightness

Whirling fruits in a blender's song,
A fruity fiesta, can't go wrong!
Each sip tickles with a burst of cheer,
We raise our cups and shout, 'Bring it here!'

Twirls of color swaying in sync,
Sipping joy, we hardly think.
Crazy flavors dance on the tongue,
In glasses tall, we sing and hum!

Cheery froth that plays in the sun,
Laughter shared is laughter won.
Giggling blends in a colorful whirl,
With each sip, we dance and twirl!

Sun-kissed droplets splash our lips,
Goofy grins and happy quips.
Here's to laughter, bright and bold,
In fruity magic, stories told!

Sunlit Serenade

Bright concoction, oh what a chore,
Mix and mash—give us more!
A fizzy laugh in a frosty cup,
Each drink a giggle—who can keep up?

Breezy flavors make us sway,
As we sip and dance all day.
Crazy fun in a fruity haze,
In golden rays, we spin and blaze!

Spoon or straw, we don't mind,
With messy hair and hugs entwined.
Joyful bliss in every taste,
Not a drop can go to waste!

Spinning around, we toast the sky,
With silly faces, oh my, oh my!
In every bubble, a story blends,
Sippin' sunshine with our friends!

Sip of Radiant Delight

Frothy top with a fruity twist,
Every sip feels like a kiss.
Giggling souls on a sunny spree,
In frosty cups, pure ecstasy!

Straws are wiggling, here and there,
Each gulp brings laughter, light as air.
Fruits parade in a silly dance,
Come take a sip, join the prance!

Colorful chaos in each blend,
Cheeky delights that twist and bend.
Together we laugh, together we sip,
In this fruity joy, we take a trip!

In every bubble, a grin unfolds,
Warmth and sweetness, the joy it holds.
Here's to laughter that never lacks,
With every sip, we're free to relax!

Velvet Gold under the Sky

In the kitchen, a dance begins,
Fruits tumble in, mixed with grins.
A splash of milk, a twist of cheer,
Laughter bubbles, the flavor's near.

Whirling blades, a fruity tornado,
Sipping dreams, far from the fado.
Golden joy in a glass so bright,
Who knew laughter would taste so right?

Straws like rockets aiming high,
Slurping fun, oh my, oh my!
It's a carnival, a cheerful bite,
Under a sky of pure delight.

With every sip, we sip the sun,
In this fruity race, we've all won.
Cheers to giggles, cheers to smiles,
A sunny day shared in joyful miles.

Morning Glow and Sweetness

The dawn arrives with playful flair,
Bright tang of fun fills the air.
A swirl of creamy, a dash of zest,
Morning giggles, we're surely blessed.

In jars of joy, sweet treasures hide,
Each sip taken with childlike pride.
A tasty whirlwind, oh what a sight,
Keeping spirits soaring and light.

Glances exchanged, as we all create,
A concoction made to celebrate.
Sunshine laughter in every pour,
More is always better, we crave more!

Cheers to the flavors that make us grin,
With each delightful sip, we win.
Smiles grow wider with each lovely glare,
Life's a party, flavors to share.

Harvest of the Sun

Fruits gathered from the summer's boon,
In a blender, they hum a tune.
Jam-packed joy, sweetness to swell,
In this wild mix, we all excel.

Whirls and swirls, what a splash,
A sip so bright, it's sure to crash.
Each gulp a giggle, a wink, a tease,
With every flavor, we aim to please.

Outdoor laughter, a bright parade,
Sipping the sunshine, all worries fade.
Chasing flavors like a playful breeze,
Caught in sweetness, our hearts feel ease.

Raise your glass to the warm embrace,
With each clink, we find our place.
Sun-kissed moments, a bright menu,
In this gathering, there's joy anew.

Chasing Warmth with Every Sip

In the morning, we find our glee,
Glorious colors, come sip with me.
Straws poised like playful probes,
Taste the fun that each blend glows.

Frothy clouds in a playful dance,
With every taste, we take a chance.
Fruits and cheer, a happy crew,
Gathering flavors, chasing the blue.

Chatter and slurps, a rhythmic beat,
Cracking jokes, it's all so sweet.
With warmth in hand, let's share a smile,
A sunlit journey, let's stay awhile.

Raise your cups, let's toast today,
To juicy moments that swirl and play.
Chasing warmth, with laughs that flip,
In every bottle, we take a trip.

Solstice Elixir

In a jar of gold, a twist of fate,
Sip it slow, let the giggles sate.
Creamy swirls, a dance in the cup,
Laughter bubbles when I drink it up.

Stirring flavors, a carnival blend,
Cheeky smiles, on that you can depend.
Fruits jive together, a wild parade,
Every sip a joke that won't ever fade.

Frothy whispers of summer's delight,
Catch the giggles, wrapped up tight.
A frosty treat, brightened gleam,
Turn your day into a silly dream.

In the shade, we clink our straws,
To this elixir, we give applause.
Jokes float around like wayward seeds,
As we chase away the daily needs.

Sweets of the Tropics

Tropical giggles, in a tall glass,
Waves of flavor, they surely amass.
Swirls of joy, on a sunny spree,
The taste of whimsy, so wild and free.

Fruits blend and bounce, a merry dance,
Dancing flavors give the tongue a chance.
Nectar of laughter, a splash in the bowl,
Pour out the happiness, let it roll.

Chillin' out while the good vibes flow,
Whiskers of fun in each happy glow.
Lemonade giggles, in a frosty rush,
Sunset promises, creating a hush.

With every sip, a smile expands,
Sweetness spreads across the lands.
Packing up joy, in this funny treat,
Cheering with every gulp, can't be beat!

Nature's Sunshine

In the morning light, with a zesty cheer,
Tasting the warmth, it's almost here.
Ticklish flavors, a party inside,
Lemonade sights, let laughter collide.

Splashing colors, a fruity delight,
Sipping happiness, everything feels right.
Slice of joy, in a fruity mess,
Every gulp, a humorous caress.

Chasing the clouds with a shiny grin,
Bliss in a cup, that's where we begin.
Whirls of sunshine take over the day,
With this playful drink, we dance and sway.

In the silly moments, we find our muse,
Giggling loudly, we simply can't refuse.
Brightened spirits in the midday glow,
With every sip, we let it all flow.

Effervescent Evenings

Under the stars with a fizzy delight,
Twinkling drinks make the mood feel right.
Bubbles of joy dance on my tongue,
In fairytale flavors, I feel so young.

Whips of sweetness mix in the air,
Creating laughter, without a care.
With each fizzy sip, we reach for the night,
A twist of fun makes everything bright.

Clinking glasses to the riff of the breeze,
Toast to the moments that put us at ease.
Witty banter mixed with fruity bliss,
Evenings alive with the magic of this.

Light-hearted smiles in every round,
Chasing the shadows, joy knows no bound.
Like fireflies glowing, we swirl and spin,
In the effervescent evening, we let the fun begin.

Luau in a Cup

A fruity feast within this glass,
Tropical tangs that make me laugh.
With every sip, the party starts,
Hula dancing in my heart.

Pineapple swirls and coconut dreams,
Laughing out loud with giggly screams.
A burst of flavor, a splash of fun,
Who knew a drink could weigh a ton?

Sipping slow, my worries drift,
This pretty drink is a magic gift.
Friends join in, we raise a cheer,
To fruity fun and no more fear!

A luau's joy wrapped up so neat,
Every sip's a sugary treat.
In my cup, good vibes collide,
A sunny smile I cannot hide.

Sweet Sunrise Serenade

Morning sunshine, oh so bright,
I squish my fruit, what a sight!
With creamy hugs and laughter near,
Each sip brings a joyful cheer.

A giggle here, a chuckle there,
Slurping loud, without a care.
Straw hats on, in silly poses,
Taste this bliss as the day dozes.

Chilled and smooth, it makes me sing,
Oh, what a joy this freshness brings!
With flavors dancing, a joke or two,
A liquid laugh, let's drink anew!

With sunshine on our silly grins,
We toast to smiles and fruity spins.
Raise your glass, let worries flee,
In sweet harmony, wild and free.

Energizing Elixirs

Blend it up, a whirl of cheer,
This potion's power is oh so clear.
With every gulp, I bounce and sway,
Kicking sleepy clouds away!

Add some laughter, sprinkle a joke,
A sip of zing, let's all provoke.
Friends gather near, with cups held high,
Feeling bubbly, we won't be shy.

Fruit flying fast, like confetti bright,
Wacky flavors, what a delightful sight!
Sipping joy in a frosty swirl,
Let's dance around and give it a twirl!

Energy bursting, can't sit still,
I'll bounce around, it's quite a thrill.
Waves of laughter, smiles so true,
With each elixir, friendships renew.

Chill of the Tropics

Caught in the chill, a frosty haze,
This colorful drink sets my heart ablaze.
Giggling with friends, we take a sip,
Sandy toes in a playful trip.

With vibrant hues swirling around,
We laugh at the mess on the ground.
Pineapple hats and coconut pearls,
This playful wonder gives me twirls.

Sunshine giggles, drifting near,
Our laughter echoes, we have no fear.
Every splash and every cheer,
This is a taste of happy here!

In our cups, the tropics thrive,
With every sip, we feel alive.
A toast to joy, silly delight,
In this fruity moment, everything's right.

Essence of Paradise

In a glass, a swirl so bright,
A yellow hug, pure delight.
Sipping through a funky straw,
I giggle at my fruity law.

Lemon laughs and berry cheers,
Dancing flavors, banish fears.
With each sip, the world seems right,
I twirl and laugh, what a sight!

The blender buzzes, a wacky tune,
As fruits unite, they start to swoon.
Whipped up chaos, colors blend,
Giggling loudly, no need to pretend.

A clumsy jug, spills here and there,
Sticky fingers, fruity fare.
In this mess, real joy is found,
In sunshine's glow, we spin around.

Cheers to Radiance

Raise your glass, make a toast,
To happy flavors we love most!
A frothy concoction, with a grin,
Chasing away the day's chagrin.

In a whirlwind of blender bliss,
A fruity mix, you can't dismiss.
Giggles bubble, juice takes flight,
Slurping loudly, oh what a sight!

Pineapple and coconut collide,
Like a party where friends reside.
With every sip, laughter grows,
A joyful drink that always flows.

Sticky laughter, spills galore,
Messy fun we can't ignore.
With sunbeams dancing on my face,
In this moment, there's pure grace.

Light and Leafy Bliss

Whirling greens with a golden hue,
A smoothie ride, oh what a view!
Taste the twirl of herb and sweet,
A giggly dance, oh what a feat!

Sip and slurp, so much delight,
Chasing sunshine with every bite.
In a glass, a joyful spree,
Laughter floats so merrily.

Chlorophyll and citrus mix,
Crafting fun with playful tricks.
A leafy party in every sip,
With energized smiles, we let it rip!

Stir the pot, create the whirl,
With vibrant flavors, we twirl and swirl.
In this concoction, joy's a bliss,
A happy moment in every kiss.

Juicy Daydreams

In a cup, wonders collide,
Fruity visions, a joyful ride.
A sip of dreams, oh so fine,
Tickles my tongue, feels divine!

With a splash of whimsy, laughs unfold,
Exotic flavors, stories told.
Dress grape in a funny hat,
Sip and shout, "How about that?"

Swirling mists of tropical spree,
Mango madness calling me.
With glee we gulp, and giggle loud,
Under a sun that makes us proud.

Sassy citrus in the mix,
A caramel twist, playtime tricks.
With each froth, pure joy we glean,
In these moments, we chase the dream!

Sunshine Reverie

A fuzzy yellow fruit rolls by,
Chasing clouds beneath the sky.
Giggles float on breezy tunes,
As laughter bubbles like balloons.

A splatter here, a splash and swirl,
Mango joins the dance, oh what a whirl!
Strawberry joins like a shy dancer,
Twisting to the rhythm's banter.

Sipping joy from a colorful cup,
Slurping up each funny hiccup.
Pulling faces with each bright treat,
Oh, what fun, oh what sweet heat!

With tiny umbrellas, sipping on bliss,
We toast to giggles and sunshine's kiss.
A party of laughter, a fruity delight,
Every sip sparkles, making life bright.

Blissful Beverages

A wild mix of colors in a glass,
Bouncing flavors, a fruity sass.
Chunks of joy, like confetti they dance,
Taking each sip, we laugh and prance.

Creamy swirls, a delightful sight,
Chasing each gulp with giddy delight.
"Oops, spilled some!" becomes our new cheer,
Sticky fingers, but no sign of fear.

Sipping slow, it's a juicy race,
Between blushing cheeks and a silly face.
Crushed ice sails like a boat on the sea,
While everyone's laughing, being silly and free.

In our fruity fort, we'll giggle and grin,
It's a blend of joy, where the fun begins.
Raise your glass, it's good vibes galore,
With each sip, we crave just a bit more!

Juicy Serenity

Fuzzy fingers dip in sweetness divine,
Pineapple pirates throw in sunshine.
A twist of lime becomes a mini show,
In the land where fruity wishes flow.

Coconut clouds float in the breeze,
As we sip joy, oh what a tease!
Mouthfuls of giggles, the fun won't stall,
Each frothy bubble brings laughter for all.

Whimsical whims splattered with cheer,
Slurping up happiness, let's all draw near.
Merry mayhem in every blend,
With giggles aplenty, there's no end.

Sipping serenely with silly delight,
We dance on the table, oh isn't it right?
Each fruity drink a delightful spree,
In this joyful blend, we're forever free!

Drenched in Delight

Sipping straws in a kaleidoscope bright,
Every drop is a burst of pure light.
Giggles erupt with each quirky blend,
As flavors collide and twist like a friend.

A splash of juice paints our faces wide,
As we chase the sweetness, we can't hide.
Giggling geysers, oh what a sight,
The messy aftermath is pure delight!

Lemonade laughter fills the warm air,
With every slurp, we forget our cares.
Sticky hands in a fruit-filled war,
Who knew drinks could be so much more?

So here's to the funny, the fruity, the fun,
In every cup, we're never done!
With smiles and flavors, we'll dance all day,
Drenched in delight, come what may!

www.ingramcontent.com/pod-product-compliance
Lightning Source LLC
Chambersburg PA
CBHW050302120526
44590CB00016B/2454